A View from the Quiet Corner

The Reflections of a Novice Poet

Alan A. Malizia

AuthorHouse™
1663 Liberty Drive
Bloomington, IN 47403
www.authorhouse.com
Phone: 1-800-839-8640

© 2009 Alan A. Malizia. All rights reserved.

No part of this book may be reproduced, stored in a retrieval system, or transmitted by any means without the written permission of the author.

First published by AuthorHouse 5/29/2009

ISBN: 978-1-4389-9108-5 (sc)

Printed in the United States of America
Bloomington, Indiana

This book is printed on acid-free paper.

Introduction

In 1994, Congress designated the Quinebaug and Shetucket Valley rivers as a Valley National Heritage Corridor, reorganizing the region as a unique national resource. In 1999, Congress enlarged the Boston, Massachusetts, to Washington, D.C., corridor with the addition of the newly combined northeastern Connecticut and south-central Massachusetts region known as "The Last Green Valley." At night, the region appears dark amid the urban and suburban lights when viewed from above. During daylight, the rural character is confirmed by green fields and forests. The 1,085-square-mile area is defined by the Quinebaug and Shetucket river systems and the rugged hills that surround them.*

Since retiring from teaching and coaching careers that spanned nearly thirty years, I have relocated to Danielson, Connecticut. Danielson is a borough of Killingly. Along with seven villages and Danielson, Killingly is the most populous community in northeastern Connecticut, commonly known as "The Quiet Corner," and is part of the aforementioned Last Green Valley.* The town of Stamford, Connecticut, which I have known since my youth, had grown into a city; a rapidly growing corporate city with a faster pace of life, congested roadways, and rising taxes alienating many of the citizens who had made Stamford their home for decades. These among other reasons encouraged the move.

In contrast, "The Quiet Corner" offers a country setting, a slower pace, and simpler joys. Its environmental attributes, which please the senses and content the soul, inspire one to put into words or depict on canvas a way of life that many have longed for but thought was lost forever. One need not return to the past to recapture those comforts of a quieter, more peaceful, secure, and serene time. One need only listen and follow the beckoning inner call that leads to those appealing areas still in existence.

The distinguishing qualities of "The Quiet Corner" did not motivate nor direct my thoughts specifically, but rather in general. The pages that follow contain my opinions on topics that I feel are relevant to all of us who may be seeking to take stock of ourselves. These opinions are expressed through original poems and reflections on each. Although each of our lives differs uniquely, there is commonality in affect, feeling, and spirit. We are influenced by many of the same things in life. Our observance, thought, and opinion on these matters are as diverse and unique as we are. Therein lies the value.

A variety of common topics can be viewed differently and worthily, based upon the perspectives of unique individuals, whether the philosopher or the dairy farmer. My hope is that those who read this book will find some value in what I have written and, by doing so, will find value in themselves.

*Information provided by "The Last Green Valley" Web site.

"A Coach's Lament"

While silently reclined
there is much that comes to mind.
Sounds and visions of seasons past
one had thought would always last.
Ghostly allies and phantom foes
embroiled in combative throes.
Bright faces of delight.
Tears, the remnants of lost fights.
Supporters' cheers
of victories won.
Moans forthcoming
as our victors' dance is done.
Hearts revealed,
no courage concealed,
as the line
was drawn.
All are fulfilled and
regrets have none,
when it's understood
what was really won.

(continues)

No mantel can hold
nor on wall be hung,
the value gained
when the battle is done.
For the prizes will character,
sacrifice, and honor be.
Yet acclaimed above all,
our camaraderie.
Forever is never
I've come to accept.
But fondness for what was
will always be kept.

Reflection

Whatever one chooses to do in life matters. In the performance of a duty or a role, happy is the person who receives a wage for performing his passion. Sadly, very often those wages are not substantial. But what price can one place on fulfillment of that passion; doing that for which you were wired? In the end, most would exchange a full portfolio for a full heart.

Unwittingly some strive for an image that is contrary to their real self. That road will eventually lead to failure. One must explore and be open to various avenues and opportunities that their true passion draws them to. In the process, let the adjustment to change happen. Don't force it. If it is suitable, in time you will know.

When you can comfortably wonder where the day has gone and look excitedly forward to more of the same, then you would have achieved your niche in life. Your compensation will be the positive effect upon family, friends, and coworkers. By exercising your gifts and realizing your passion you in turn will help others find their niche.

I majored in mathematics in college. After graduating I pursued a dream career in the aerospace field. When the dream became a nightmare I wondered and wandered. Finally, I received a gentle push from my mother that transformed into a stumble toward coaching youngsters. That joyful experience led to a rewarding career as a mathematics teacher and high school athletics coach.

I have since retired from both. However, I look back on my experiences with a fullness and satisfaction that no other profession or endeavor could have produced. My failure to achieve the false want in reaching for the stars became the successful achievement of the true need found in the hearts of the children I taught and coached.

It is inevitable that all things, good and bad, come to an end. But in quoting, "It is better to have loved and lost than never to have loved at all," we can understand that the same can be concluded about one's inherent passion; his or her niche. For those who never love are truly lost, and a niche found is secured for life. Even at life's end the satisfaction and peace of heart is yours forever. Wherever one's passion lies there also will be his attention, energy, and love.

"My All Hallows Eve"

An autumn eve has fallen.

Through my window I gaze entranced.

Wisps of gossamer clouds propelled by gentle winds intermittently mask the features of a harvest moon.

These passing veils are perceived as ghostly apparitions to the active imagination.

A lone passerby with hurried gait comes into view, directing my thoughts from the moment to a past experience.

My senses are triggered by

The sound of dried fallen leaves compressed between foot and ground.

The rustle of the same, stampeding, rushing along the earthen surface empowered by an Indian summer breeze.

My calm trance is broken by a knock at the door.

As I release the latch the portal opens on creaking hinges, giving evidence of inattention.

I'm startled by this eventful eve's reminder.

(continues)

There before me are assembled a variety of the unworldly.

Each one individual, yet common in their pursuit of confectionary delights.

As my satisfied visitors depart

I slowly close the door.

Giving pause, I reluctantly let go of this eerie yet pleasant silence and serenity that is unique to this magical night.

Reflection

Regardless of its origin or religious and cultural significance, Halloween, from the viewpoint of the young, has always been anticipated as an exciting evening of mystery and fun. The fun experienced in the past has been wholesome while interspersed with a little harmless mischief.

When I was a child our family lived in a housing project. Residency requirements were based on one's particular financial status. Once a family's income breached to the upside it was necessary to find a new home within a designated period of time. All the families in the project were in the same financial boat, but not the same ethnic boat. The breadwinners of the household were blue-collar workers who made ends meet with the help of other family members pitching in.

What made the holiday unique in comparison to others is that it was community centered as opposed to family centered. The large number of families provided a multitude of youthful trick-or-treaters. All sorts of costumed ghosts, goblins, princesses, clowns, hobos, and yes, even a smattering of saints roamed the neighborhood from dusk until midnight with candy sacks in hand.

What a great time it was, in the chronological sense. A time in our personal histories allowing a magical evening for youngsters with imaginative wonderings to briefly role-play a hero, a hope, or a dream free from fears of reprisal. It was a refreshing time, encouraged by a commonality of hard work, consideration, and simple pleasures.

"A Circle's Testimony"

Without a beginning
and without an end.
No known start or finish
is distinguished within its bend.
From one point radiates
precision in all directions.
Creating the curve
that is perfect without exception.
Its functions are many
if time is taken to observe.
By circumference, area, and volume
a portion of its purpose is served.
Finite and infinite,
impossible yet true.
For the constant within
is incalculable.

(continues)

The fact that it exists
with such conflicting attributes,
makes one wonder:
From whence comes its roots?
Its roots? It has none.
Because it always was.
For man can only discover
as a human being does.
How then did this unique figure
of geometry come to be?
From that which has its same nature;
who was, is now, and will always be.

Reflection

I have always appreciated the precision and conciseness of mathematics in a world of uncertainty. I learned more about and from mathematics as a teacher than I did as a student or programmer. Precision makes mathematics unique among all the other disciplines studied. Absent are the grey areas that foster doubt until a final truth is revealed, reinstating its black-and-white status.

In our world there are physical laws that govern the very large (universe) and the very small (atoms, quarks, etc.). Mathematicians and physicists for decades have been in search of a "unifying equation" that would harmoniously bridge the two contrasting worlds. Until now research has led to some interesting theories, but theories nonetheless.

For an observable event to exist there must have been cause. It is for this cause that these dedicated professionals search. The underlying argument among reasoning men and women is whether all that we know of was born of chance or design. Our large and small worlds are uniquely quite complex in their makeup, to say the least. Was it an accident that caused all to be or an orchestration? A simple exercise in probability should shed some light.

Let's suppose we place a white marble in a container. What would be the likelihood of successfully retrieving the white marble on the first draw? One out of one, or

100 percent, of course. Now let's slightly complicate the experiment by returning the white marble to the container along with a black one. As we attempt to retrieve the white marble from the container on the first draw we now find our likelihood of success to be one out of two, or 50 percent. If we continue complicating the experiment by adding more and more black marbles to the one white one we find the probable outcome of successfully choosing the white one on the first draw less and less likely with each added black. If the container were large enough to hold the lone white marble and 999,999 black we can conclude that on first draw the chance of successfully choosing the white marble to be one in one million (1/1,000,000).

This has been an exercise in testing chance. Each added black marble increased the complexity of the experiment rendering the desired outcome quite improbable. This experiment pales in comparison when considering the complexities inherent in our large and small physical worlds. I now ask you to reconsider the original argument posed in light of the results of our experiment. One would have to agree that a strong case cannot be made for chance over design.

"A Peace I've Known"

My preoccupation. My distress.
My impatience. My duress.
My discontent. My imbalance.
All that is unsettling to one.
It is all before me in a busy thoroughfare,
a hectic workplace, a home.
In the demands of those loved and those tolerated.
Draining energy, time, and spirit.
As the walls of life close in, as often
is permitted, I search for a place.
A place of solitude and silence
where sense overcomes the senseless.
There is such a place I can go to
that restores hope and equilibrium.
A place recalled by my senses
and forever rooted in my mind.
There my blurred vision becomes clear
as I view moonlight,
dancing over a vast, perpetual,
undulating ocean.

(continues)

My hearing is sharpened as the sounds
of the chaotic, animate, and inanimate,
are replaced by the soothing, endless rhythm
of foaming surf beating against the shore.
Waves, like grasping, liquid hands
attempt to hold onto the beach
as moist granules of sand
slip through its watery fingers.
The effort is in vain as moon's force
lures it back to its depths.
Still, I find my heart in step
with its rhythm.
The gentle balmy breezes, scented by the sea's fragrance,
softly caresses my cheek as that of a lover,
and enfolds me as once did the arms of my mother.
Comforting sounds abound thanks to rustling palm branches.

At this moment I feel stress and tension rush out of me.
The vacuum left is now occupied by a sigh of contentment.
I hesitate to move for fear of losing
this rarity of unique peace.

The silence of the night is broken by the mournful sound

of a tanker's horn, off in the distance.
The gentle distraction only enhances
this most pleasant experience.
To further my delight, some miles down the shoreline,
where eye can see yet ear cannot hear,
a thunderstorm rages.
Nature's own fireworks display.

With each bolt of lightning the sky flickers with
sporadic brightened intensity, revealing the cloud
formations customarily hidden by night's darkness.

I am freely in awe of this event,
for my proximity negates any fear.
It is a fortunate I who can conjure up as desired this
most vivid calm.
So precious a moment it is
when God lifts this world's confining veil,
giving one a joyous glimpse of heaven.

Reflection

When we advance with age, we are daily confronted with adult problems. These problems may be employment or home-related. The workday extends rather than shortens, unexpectedly so, for one who has invested many years on the job. Age and experience should have their advantages, but not in our competitive world where a pat on the back is soon followed by, "What have you done for me lately?" Professional demands become increasingly burdensome. This reality is due, in part, to a lack of youthful resilience and energy that was present in our earlier lives.

We question the place in which we find ourselves. The challenges of each day should be fewer and less intense. At workday's end we return home with hope of rejuvenating solitude. This hope soon eludes us, however, as we are greeted with domestic upheavals that have been building momentum while we were at work. Whether it be backed-up plumbing or a request from Junior's teacher to discuss his habitual poor behavior in class, all must be addressed immediately.

It matters not if one is single or married, living alone or with others. The ever-present demands, either self-imposed or not, compel us to seek escape if only through memory of our most contented past experiences when problems were not ours but our parents' or, at least, that of some other poor soul. In this rare, quiet moment, we find solace in a special place and blissful peace from a time less complicated where all is still, joyous, and just makes sense.

"Control"

The pitcher's toss, whether strike or ball,
is left to the judgment of the umpire's call.
The golfer's swing with all motions' parts to be met;
will the final result be joy or regret?

The weather's forecast may be better served
by an open window where the truth is observed.
The roll of the dice, a draw from the deck.
Odds are in favor of luck at best.
What lies around the bend if could be foretold,
may well be what the future will hold.
If one bobbed instead of weaved or left a second sooner than late.
The watched pot, as we wait and wait.
Whether with good intentions or evil intent,
through best-laid plans
our wasted energies
are spent.

One's unexpected departure
or an infant's first stroll.
Of this and so much more
we have no control.
Only attitude toward all
is of what we have hold.
To accept, find humor in,
or simply let go.

Reflection

By definition, control is to have power over, restraint, or influence as in directing an experiment or reducing the severity of an event by incorporating suitable controls. Of the various meanings given, the one of most interest and desired is to have power over. This power if it could be relied upon would see all our dreams come true and all our ventures succeed without a hitch. However, we all know this is not the case. No matter how well we plan or what measures we take we can only anticipate so many of the "what-ifs" that lie before us that intend to disrupt the realization of our dreams.

When we have control we are content. When we don't we are frustrated and fearful. Anyone who pursues goals will agree that control over the influences of our lives is temporary and fleeting. The most telling statement that comes to mind and confirms control's rarity is "What happened?" What happened to that sweet cooperative offspring of mine now having become a teenager? What happened to that two-to-one favored-to-win thoroughbred that carried our next month's mortgage payment over the finish line dead last.

I know that these and many examples, humorous or not, can be discouraging. But one can take heart, for there are some things over which we do have control. Despite the pitfalls that threaten our dreams and plans we still have control over what we dream and how we plan. And to combat the pitfalls we can use our ability to adjust to ensure that our plan to successfully achieve our dream moves forward.

We must be cautious in our relentless pursuit of control over the uncontrollable. In the process we may very likely lose control of ourselves. We must also be aware that control secured by one may depend upon another relinquishing theirs. To ensure that the things that are governed by Murphy's Law do not overwhelm us but remain in the shadows, we must exercise the one guaranteed control in life we have, that which is over our attitude.

"Grandma's Presence"

When you were born
you brought such light.
It transformed any darkness
into days so bright.
New arrivals will
do that, you know.
As we make an account
of each finger and toe.
As you advanced in years
with achievement or not,
in my heart you've always
held a very special spot.
How proud I was of you, despite
what odds against might arise.
Still you held fast to truth
while others followed lies.
As now you await
your little one too,
I hope you realize
I'm as excited as you.
I have no doubt
what a great mother you'll make.

For you possess the gift
that this awesome task will take.
You're kind, warm, giving,
and steadfast too.
But loving is the most important
that you will have to do.
Rest assured I haven't missed
a step along the way.
And I will be present
on that most eventful day.
Love doesn't end with absence
as some believe, you know.
It's the only thing
we can take from this world.
And it continues to grow.

Reflection

Originally I had written this poem for my niece who was expecting her first child. My mom, her grandmother, had just passed away and would not be present for the birth of her great-grandchildren. As I reflected upon the poem I began to see meaning beyond what I had intended. What follows are my thoughts born of that meaning.

My mom and dad brought my two older brothers and me into this world. In observing how they handled the difficulties life did bring in its various forms and untimeliness I can conclude they were realistically prepared and grounded in faith. I believe a common question often pondered in our present time is "Why conceive children?" This is based upon our culture's quest to avoid anything that can be potentially unpleasant. Very few see value in struggle. When considering the evidence of poor parenting observed, it might be advisable for some couples to adhere to the above question. However, be that as it may, let us focus on those who are ready for parenthood yet have seemingly valid concerns, providing, of course, that the physically demanding aspects of the birth process will not be potentially life threatening to either mother or child.

By bringing children into this world one would not only be exposing these innocents to the beautiful wonders of this world, but also to the numerous guaranteed threats and hardships of life. The latter is their argument against conceiving. Furthermore, our children will in time be burdened with the knowledge of their mortality. By giving them life, essentially we assure their death as was accomplished on Calvary. Despite the unpleasant aspects to be faced, the value in having children can be twofold; uniqueness and love.

Once a process begins, as in the case of conception, the uniqueness of the child's potential exists regardless of the outcome. The child is a part of an eternally continuous process initiated by divine love. This uniqueness confirms that each of us is one of a kind and has but one opportunity to exist.

It is inevitable that in the course of our lives we will experience unwanted hardships, one of which is loss, loss of a relationship, a way of life, or in the death of a loved one. None of us is immune. The greatest loss I believe is the last mentioned. At this dreaded moment sadness, distress, and despair engulf us. One cannot fathom carrying on without the one lost. How is one to overcome challenges or enjoy good fortune in the future in the absence of that reassuring strength and celebratory confidant once relied upon? These moments are now strangely unfamiliar because of the void left by that former unique presence. Life can't go on as we knew it because it will no longer be as we knew it.

Yet life can continue, and successfully so. There will be joy and sorrow to come. During these periods we will be encouraged to pensively pause and remember those, now absent, who loved us enough to put aside all natural selfish concerns and give us the opportunity to love them and others, to be loved by them and others, and to love and be loved by God. And once we come to know that love of God, all the imperfections of the world fade away and we will have fulfilled our purpose, to be supremely happy. Therefore, we honor and validate those who chose to give us life and know they are always with us as integral parts of God's ongoing creation.

"He"

He arrives as a thief
in the night.
With no compassion
for one's concern or fright.
He infiltrates
quite slow.
Being invaded,
one would never know.

Control is his motive
and one of his intents.
As you are forced to grapple
with diminishing strength.
Now that he is in,
he does his dirty deed.
Selfish parasitic ravaging
is his solitary need.
He possesses neither
mind, spirit, nor soul.
He only is; with a purpose.
To steal what God has sewn.

(continues)

You're stopped in your tracks,
with barely a muscle to move.
your new stage has been set
by this villainous ghoul.

While you linger with senses
dulled and quite out of tune.
Enters a thought:
Will my life end all too soon?

A revelation comes forth
at a time such as this.
All things taken for granted
will regretfully be missed.
If given the chance
I'd accept things as things be.
Instead of the whimsical
wishes of me.
Now with struggle as catalyst
I see all the better.
Sadly, nature's overlooked beauty
may be lost to me forever.

My hearing is the best
it has ever been.
Not just to the sounds around me,
but presumed voices of family and friends.
My assumptions are fewer.
My awareness has grown.
This credit is given
to the he I have known.
For the fortunate me
who survives his attack.
Another day I'll see
and self-centeredness will I lack.
While on pain's course
one wonders at first
would death itself
have truly been worse?
But as time moves on
it heals all wounds.
This death cannot accomplish.
Only God's gift will exhume.

Reflection

Disease is our enemy; the battlefield our bodies. In conventional warfare the purpose of the enemy is to render his opponent defenseless and thereby lay claim to his land and possessions and thereby alter his life as he knows it. The victors will strive to maintain their hold over the spoils gained. Disease, if it doesn't kill, can physically and mentally change the quality of life for its victim's natural term. The battle wages and rages at times each day. The disabled are constantly under siege when faced with what would be considered unnoticeable obstacles by the able bodied. Staircases, narrow paths and doorways, unkept thoroughfares, or a slippery floor are unseen skirmishes by most. Just the struggle getting in and out of bed at day's beginning and end reminds one of the enemy's presence and discomforting legacy.

When faced with lasting turmoil the victim may, in time, not only be physically, mentally, and emotionally worn but spiritually tested as well. To avoid this he must learn to function successfully while engaged in the relentless battle. In war, to regain strength, re-evaluate the situation, and devise new strategies one's forces would retreat behind protective defensive lines. Likewise victims of disease must do the same. Find places of solitude and momentarily let go of the battle; regenerate, re-assess, and prepare for what the enemy may further have in store.

These temporary retreats may to some seem like resignation. Instead it is rejuvenating reflection. In this way one can stay in the unavoidable fight and in the end emerge victorious; victorious not only in battle but in the war through perseverance fueled by faith. The opinions and thoughts on this matter are offered by one who has been in the trenches and daily must manage the ongoing effects of post-polio syndrome. Some years ago I spoke to my local P.P.S. support group. In my talk I provided some enlightenment to questions that have been personally persistent.

I've come to understand that winning is not success and losing is not failure. Success is fighting the good fight and seeing the race to its end.* Failure is not stepping up to the line at all.

I've come to understand that a parent's love is forever. It is our bond with them and sustains us even in their absence.

I've come to understand that those who chose to befriend me also took on my disability as theirs. Two or more shouldering the same cross lightens the burden considerably.

I've come to understand that we polio survivors are a unique fellowship. For God's gift to Dr. Jonas Salk assures a potential future devoid of polio victims, thereby one day bringing our fellowship to an end.

How might our fellowship be remembered when the last of us is gone? The legacy could read as follows: There once was a group of people who were innocent victims of a faceless, ruthless evil that is no more. A people who although challenged daily with physical, mental, and emotional hardships held fast and stayed their chosen courses that led to successful and fulfilled lives. A people whose twofold gift to all was that hope is inherently good yet leaves room for doubt and that faith alone ensures that the imaginable and unimaginable become truth.

*Adapted from 1 Timothy 1:18 and 2 Timothy,4:7.

"My Why of Suffering"

Pain and suffering I have,
for which I asked not.
Daily things others take for granted,
are the added chores that I've got.

When I rise in the morning
with muscles and joints stiff,
my focusing eyes
look to He who on cross is fixed.
Just in reach
and under His place
are my aluminum crutch
and leather-strapped brace.
As I don my equipment
I think of Him too.
How great was the trial
He had to go through.

(continues)

Despite the strife, angst,
and ridicule of many,
He carried out His purpose
not second to any.
On any given day when
my complaints may be many.
He continued to give
as His life force reached empty.
At the end of my day,
I remove crutch and brace
and routinely return them
to their night's place.
I again raise my eyes
to His place on the wall.
First I wonder, Why?
Then realize He did it
for the good of us all.

My struggle, I thought,
might have value too.
If not for the many,
then at least for a few.
For one to be observed
in how he handles his plight,
a conclusion is drawn; in spite of it all,
he has done all right.

The task itself is quite troublesome,
yet well worth the effort
if just one viewing soul
wills to push on.
So as I lie down to rest
I can fervently attest.
He and I both,
have done our very best.
With me in my bed
and He up above,
at last I've found
my answer to suffering.
It's an expression of love.

Reflection

There are two things in life we know for sure. We were born and we will die. Between entrance and exit we will experience physical, emotional, and spiritual comfort and suffering. With comfort we have no grievance. Few would lodge a complaint against the pleasure received from good food and beverage, companionship of loving family and friends, and the most cherished moments of sensual peace and contentment. Only when all that influence our personal world, be they of nature or man, give us their best sides do we receive those welcome joys.

But as sure as there is comfort so also there is suffering. Everything has its season. The good and the bad will have theirs. Those who think otherwise are deceiving themselves. Negative influences can and will show their worst sides. The effect will not be that characterized by longed-for pleasures. Rather we will be recipients of pain and discomfort that are capable of bringing forth the worst of our natures in the expression of doubt, frustration, and anger. All surface from within us, through the portal of fear. There are those who will regress to despair if the extent and duration of suffering are extreme. Our human tendency is to place inordinate value on comfort and render suffering valueless. Who wouldn't choose pleasure over pain? So then what purpose is there in suffering?

Suffering exists due to the absence of comfort. Since we experience each we can evaluate each. One couldn't truly appreciate comfort or pleasure unless having had pain and suffering to compare. What value would there be in light if not for contrasting darkness? Therein lies a purpose for suffering, and not necessarily a positive one. Can there be a positive aspect of suffering?

Let's investigate two examples of individuals, each burdened with a physical malady. The first responds as most would expect, quite negatively, desperately wishing for the restored comfort and strength he had taken for granted. In time he succumbs to despair as loved ones helplessly and hopelessly look on.

On observing our second individual it is obvious that he had not placed pleasure and comfort on the top pedestal in his life. Realizing good times would not endure forever he enjoyed and appreciated them while they lasted. Now he fears less and comes to understand suffering. After an initial lapse into self-pity this sufferer begins the fight to find a solution regardless of the outcome. With little complaint or anger through an accepting attitude, fear and frustration are kept at bay and despair at a distance. He will be victorious no matter the outcome, for he is nurtured and rooted in the stuff that ensures endurance of the test. Balance is maintained. Loved ones standing by in this case are rewarded with hope and strength and are uplifted by his inspiring example and remedy to suffering.

Which observing group then will be better prepared for their inevitable confrontation with suffering? One will be inclined to despair while the other hope. What is at stake is saving or losing one's soul. If our love is first and foremost for our own well-being then we would agree with the first approach. Essentially that is to give up. If we hold the well-being of others first and foremost then we would agree with the second. That is to hold on.

Herein lies a purpose and value in suffering. Through it we are given the opportunity to inspire rather than discourage; to save souls or not. And in saving others perhaps we in turn save ourselves.

"The Maze"

We enter this life with a purpose,
as a mouse in a maze.
Not a temporary experiment,
but one that lasts all our days.
Our rodent friend
has but one goal in his mind,
to stay the twisting course
until the prize he does find.
He is relentless in pursuit
and unfettered by what blocks his way.
For he is driven by something from within.
Which makes us both somewhat the same.

In one respect, we are most different
from our diminutive friend.
While he holds fast to the goal,
it's giving up that we tend.
Why do we give in, though the goal be in sight?

(continues)

Is it the endless meandering turns
or life's distractions
that diminish our fight?
Our maze expert displays
that desire, patience, and stamina are what is needed.
Not satisfaction from instant solutions
by which progress and purpose are impeded.

So from our little friend,
let us learn a valuable lesson.
Goals great or small can only be achieved
by steadfast determination.

Reflection

I'm sure that in one form or another we've all heard someone, if not ourselves, make the statement "I want my children to have an easier time in growing up than I." Although the intentions are well meaning, this need to spare our children from struggle in the end may be their undoing. Allowing the young experiences with struggle instills and strengthens resolve. This is a necessary ingredient to guard against quitting when the road gets a bit bumpy.

Let us revisit the story of "the prodigal son" and take it a step further for those familiar with the parable as told by Jesus. A father had two sons. The younger of the two asked for his part of the inheritance, now. His father granted his request, and the younger son was on his way. In little time he had squandered every bit of the money on wanton frivolous living and succumbed to all sorts of temptations. He was reduced to the life of a beggar and had to settle for the food scraps left by swine for nourishment. He realized that his only way to survive was to swallow his pride and return home. He would offer himself as a slave and labor in the fields. For even as a slave he would be fed, sheltered, and clothed. So he set off for home.

His father on seeing him approach went out to greet him. He was so pleased to see his son again that he embraced him, dressed him in fine clothes, adorned him with jewelry, and celebrated his return with a lavish party.

His older son, who had always been faithful and obedient, was upset because he for all his hard work and dedication had never been rewarded in the least. We know the end of the parable and the lesson: "Rejoice, for your brother was lost and is found again. He was dead and now lives." It is about redemptive forgiveness.

Let's view the story from the perspective of the older son. On the surface it seems he's gotten the proverbial short end of the stick. However, this is not so. His father reassures him that his loyalty has not gone unnoticed. "You are with me always, and all that I have is yours." His inheritance (reward) is as real as it has always been. Yet it is of more value to him than his brother because it was gained through effort and struggle, not an unearned windfall. It will endure, grow, and not be lost to wanton squandering. Struggle has fortified him against the temptation to take the path most traveled as his brother did.

The road to a successful life, whether temporal or eternal, is not that taken by the prodigal son. The true value in achievement can only be measured by the level of struggle in attaining it. Life truly is a maze, for those who seek the easy route may likely be confronted by endless dead ends. But for those who pursue with patience, persistence, and perseverance the end eventually will be in sight. And what a sight to behold!

"The Lure"

In elemental bliss meandering effortlessly by current's force.

Nourished by nature's gifts and in playful wonder.

Investigating the curious while darting about and around

Subterranean flora and stone.

What distractive presence diverts attention

From aquatic joy?

Luminous bauble entrances

And draws from fellowship's security.

A close nudge brings no response

From the bright enticement.

Unwarranted confidence

Compels the bite.

What force has hold?!

Instinct's flight or fight takes charge!

Adrenaline-inspired muscles contract and expand violently

Giving rise to raging foam of freedom's frantic battle.

(continues)

Fruitless resistance
Merely retards predestined fate.
Oh cherished world removed!
Comforter and protector lie beneath.

Desperation's last surge is for naught.
Unknown light's reflector
Inextricably binds
And has its way.

Earth's foreign element restricts.
Hampered respiration
And mounting fatigue
Transforms resolve to resignation.
Oh, wanton and regretful eye
Having accepted deceit's invitation
Now fades to the vision
Of winged counterpart in elemental bliss.

Reflection

Our world is filled with an almost endless abundance of attractions, some of which are of a very positive nature and enhance our lives. More often than not the positive value of these attractions is validated by benefits indirectly received by others around us. The attraction between man and woman blossoms into a loving, committed, understanding, and durable marriage. The offspring of this couple will be nurtured and influenced in such a way that they too are likely to carry on those same attributes in the relationships they develop in life.

Occupational attractions will ensure that the vocations we are called to suit us. Our satisfaction and fulfillment we experience when we perform the work we have a gift for will pay dividends not only for us but for coworkers and family as well. Our contentment and joy will enhance their lives as the environment shared by all will be enjoyable. Those affected will also be motivated to follow their hearts and minds to those attractions that will satisfy their unfulfilled gifts. There are attractions that will sufficiently satisfy want also.

There is a difference between want and need. When need is satisfied it is enough for the individual. Want is never fully satisfied. Need and want have one thing in common. They are both temporal. However, temporal satisfaction of need can last a lifetime, while in the case of want there may not be enough lifetimes. We've all heard the saying "The grass grows greener on the other side." This is the golden rule of want. No possession or accomplishment is enough to satisfy. The disciples of want have an insatiable appetite for more. They cannot be content or joyous because they have not given their attention to the attractions of the heart and soul. Instead they are solely committed to sense and mind.

The person who has experienced the joy of fulfilled need and understands that all things of this world are fleeting will not be angered or resentful when those things are no more. He has a lasting appreciation for that unique human summit if realized even for only a moment.

On the other hand our friend who has lost all that he wanted will not be gracious at all. He frantically will search to fill the void with other mundane substitutes. The nature of this parasite is not to exist in and of himself. He has never recognized the infinite potential of a full heart and soul. He has only known the temporary quenches of sense and mind. His substance-less addiction to want has trapped him in a vicious circle that in the end if remaining unaltered may lead to his eventual destruction.

"Resilient Pond"

Mirrored liquid calm.
Canvas for inverted pastel flora
Beautifully haloed in azure.
Once still membrane
Penetrated by minute-like kin
From above.
Ever-increasing turbulence
Fosters obscurity.
Disfigured surface
Transforms known to unknown.
With passing time's patience
The disrupter departs.
Ebb and flow subside
Under nature's steady grip.
With decreasing undulation
The familiar visage reappears
To the joy of the beholder.

Reflection

Why is it that at the most comfortable, secure, and serene episodes of our lives the unexpected happens? There are those who are prepared for these disruptive if not life-changing events and those who are not. Those who habitually harbor dark memories of the disharmonies they've experienced are constantly looking back, wishing those misfortunes had never happened. The longer these negative attitudes are held onto the deeper entrenched they become. While forever looking over their shoulders they never see ahead the wall they are about to slam into. That wall may be no greater a burden than the one left behind on which their eye is fixed. However, it is perceived as such or more because the undiscarded load of bad past experiences eventually crushes the carrier. The one straw too many will do its damage if not purged.

Others have learned much from their past life misfortunes, if only to just leave them there. They recognize the signs of the impending storm before it's upon them and are prepared. After gaining the knowledge to ensure future-needed solutions they need not look back to a no-longer-useful past and are therefore free to focus on what is ahead. No clung-to weight of bad experiences will put them at a disadvantage as they deal with future unexpected events. A ship in a storm must be trimmed and sometimes lightened by tossing overboard the nonessential cargo to weather the storm and salvage what good remains and the very vessel itself.

Those who choose to learn from the difficulties in life and then discard them as no longer useful will have prepared themselves to weather any storm in life. With light burdens their stability will be maintained until the difficulty passes. Also, they will be well equipped to successfully manage the challenging aftermath, allowing a familiar calm to return. This is so because those who have loosed excess baggage and are rooted in their convictions will not allow self-imposed demons to weaken their foundation.

"Undeserved Blemish"

With nearness the countenance becomes clear.
Purity untouched by corruption
As modesty shrouds the head.

Configuration of the mouth divulges naught.
While the eyes reveal all-knowing truth.

Eyes piercing, yet placid.
Commanding, yet comforting.
Inviting the jaded and confused
As much as the avid and lucid.
The solitary blemish witnessed gently rolling down silken cheek is a crimson tear.
Shed for the likes of me.

Reflection

In my autobiography, *The Little Red Chair*, I tell of a childhood experience that took place in the summer of 1960 when I was ten years old. It was reported that a picture of the Blessed Mother of Jesus had shown evidence of tears. The picture was one of two icons owned by a Long Island, New York, husband and wife. The event was first witnessed in their home.

After scientific scrutiny and validation by Greek orthodox hierarchy, its authenticity was confirmed. At the request of Fr. Poulos, pastor of the Church of the Archangels in Stamford, Connecticut, the picture was loaned to the church for public viewing.

Accompanied by my parents and relatives I attended an evening service and veneration. At the conclusion of the service all were invited to view the icon, which was mounted on a pedestal near the altar. When I reached the front and was the next viewer an attendant tipped the pedestal forward so I could get a better look. As a result of polio I wore full-length leg braces and crutches and could not negotiate the step that separated me from the picture. I scanned all parts of the picture with youthful wonder.

When all present departed to their means of transportation home I overheard those in my party discussing what they had just experienced. To my surprise none had seen anything out of the ordinary, not even evidence of wetness. I was perplexed. Why hadn't they seen the red glistening tear drops of blood clearly visible, at least to me, on the image's cheek?

Forty-five years later I would embark on a personal pilgrimage. Two of the three icons in existence were enshrined at St Paul's Cathedral in Long Island. One, entitled *The Lamenting Panagia* (*Our Lady of Sorrows*), was the picture I viewed in my youth and was the catalyst for my pilgrimage. Fr. Poulos was helpful in finding its whereabouts.

One day in 2005, with my friend Steve, I made my pilgrimage. The day was clear and crisp as we reached our destination. The cathedral was beautiful and Byzantine-like in architecture. The interior was adorned ornately with statues, stained-glass windows, and tiled depictions of biblical events. In the far left front were two marble pedestals. Encased in each, under protective glass, were the icons. I could only approach to within fifteen to twenty feet of them in their shadowed location. My wheelchair could not advance beyond the narrow stairs leading to the icons. Steve located a person from maintenance who used a flashlight in an effort to illuminate the area. I was able, with his help, to see the picture in the improved lighting. I recognized the image of the lady as seen at the church in Stamford. Steve, being in better position than I, was able to inspect the icon at close range. He did agree that there was evidence of past wetness. From my vantage point I could not be as sure. I asked about red teardrops. He saw nothing of that nature.

As we traveled home, Steve expressed his regrets that I couldn't get a better view of the picture. I had struggled with the idea of making the trip for years, thinking that perhaps it was best to leave the image etched in the mind of the child (me) undisturbed. I knew that no matter how close my proximity to the icon or how well lighted the viewing area I would have seen the same as my friend, if that. For I looked upon her face with the aged eyes of one influenced by the realities of life that encourage doubt, rather than the youthful eyes of innocent faith-filled expectation.

"The Guardian"

I've provided crimson and gold
contrast to the autumn blue sky.
My solitary purpose is
to be pleasing to your eye.
Birds of the air
seeking respite from flight
find my appendages inviting
on which to light.
As breezes gently rock me
it inspires winged song.
Which is soothing to your ear
and diminished all you found wrong.
Under leaf-filled limbs you sought comfort
from the summer sun's rays
and umbrella-like protection
when a sudden storm raged.
Excitedly you swung high
and picnicked beneath.
I supported you as counter
in hide and go seek.
You've gathered around me
to photo the highlights of life.

Among them the arrival
of each new little tyke.
As age crept upon you,
with the aid of a woodland friend,
you were safely cradled between us
by a hammock that did extend.
Final darkness has fallen
as you endlessly sleep.
Rest assured my branches enfold you,
as my vigil I keep.

Reflection

We depend upon so much and so many in our lives. More often than not we either lack knowledge of or appreciation for them. That is likely because the most worthwhile support and protection is derived from silent steadfast benefactors who choose to remain in the shadows. Their purpose is to serve, safeguard, and direct us through the early stages of life; tweaking, prodding, and encouraging where necessary. Included among their tasks is to steer their charges toward that which will foster good health, happiness, and fulfillment as well as respect for others' hopes and dreams.

They impress upon our minds that all the good we attain is born of our own initiative so as to ensure future self-motivation and confidently taking up the gauntlet of challenges yet to come. They stand by and observe how their influence in our growth and development has transformed us into self-sufficient and sustaining individuals. At this point our clandestine guides recede further in range so as not to inspire an inkling that their masked efforts should be held responsible in any way for the wholesome wholeness of our station.

As we advance in years, knowledge and hopefully the wisdom of our unknown mentors who have placed themselves behind the scenes are brought forth through our matured awareness, appreciation, and understanding of their nonself-serving acts. We recognize their selfless sacrifice and suppression of ego as they guided us by love. Lessons learned we now apply to those impressionable lives left in our care. For we pass on what was bequeathed to us. The valued goodness and truth that were once integral to our successful development are now dispensed by us as guardians.

"Finding One's Home"

Faces and places that once defined
Me are left behind.
The contrasts of the Me
and the I are revealed.
The Me trying to hold fast
to the familiar
as the I attempts to let go
in pursuit of an unknown.
An unexplained restlessness deep within
drives the heart in search of home.
If home is where the heart is,
why is it so troubled?
Was there not comfort, joy,
Peace, and sanctuary where I resided?
Therein lies the conflict
of the Me and the I.
On life's carousel
the Me is content to cling
to its steed as the ride
runs its course.
The I opposingly relinquishes
the security of saddle and reign

while reaching for the brass ring.
The struggle is unavoidable.
For the Me and the I are of the same.
The Me must undergo the discomfort
and angst of change
as the I with its uncontrollable
need to fill the emptiness
moves forward with the quest.
The irony of this endless turmoil
between the Me and I is that the void
can only be completely filled by going home.
Home where both are truly one.

Reflection

As young children at play with our peers full attention is given to the moment. Suddenly during overzealous play one may be accidentally injured. Immediately induced is a redirection of attention to home; home where resides Dad, the provider and protector, and Mom, the nurturer and comforter. Home where all is safe and secure.

On one occasion, as most slighted children have done at one time or another, I announced that I was leaving home. Rather than receiving the sympathy I had expected, my mom asked if I would require a lunch. So with that for motivation I was on my way. I could hear the muffled smattering of giggles in the background from my siblings who were present. The reason for not taking me too seriously was not the lack of affection or concern, but instead the thought of how far I would get on two crutches and two full leg braces.

To their surprise and mine I made it around the corner and out of sight. I was determined to show them. While walking, reason began to diminish a bit of the steam from my engine that had originally fueled my mission. The further I distanced myself from the front door of my home the more I wanted to return. Even though I would have to swallow my pride and put up with some "I told you so's," I headed back. For my home was always a place of fun, comfort, security, and love. It's where I wanted to be. As I made the turn that would bring my home into view, there walking toward me were my brothers, the three of us so different yet common in our love, support, and protection of each other. They were sent by my parents to bring me home. Whatever my initial motivation was to leave, it wasn't strong enough to resist the call to return. Being away from my family left me incomplete. Their certainty of my return must have faded, for my brothers were sent in search of me. My guess is home might have been incomplete without me as well.

On this topic of finding home I think one of the best examples I've come across was from an excerpt from the book published by Ignatius Press titled *Through the Years With Fulton Sheen,* compiled and edited by Henry Dieterich. Bishop Sheen's insight and unique story-telling has brought Christian teachings to many in a new light of understanding. The story that follows, I feel, best fits the personal experience I've discussed above. It is titled: "A missing piece of your heart."

This human heart of yours is not perfect in shape as a Valentine heart. There's a small piece missing out of the side of your heart and every human heart. That is the piece that was torn out of the universal heart of humanity on the cross. When God made your heart and every other heart, He found it so good that He kept a small sample of it in heaven and then sent the rest of it into this world where it would try to fill up all the love it could, but where it would never really be happy, never totally in love, never able to love anyone with a whole heart, because it hasn't a whole heart to love with. It will never be happy until it goes back to God to recover that piece that He has been keeping for it from all eternity. To go home.

"Conclusion"

In my retirement and through the influences of my new surroundings, those distractions, both enjoyed and not, that were a part of my former life circumstances no longer are a hindrance to the depth of reflection and evaluation that I can give to the experiences I have had. Hopefully conclusions drawn will be for the better.

Throughout our lives we are faced with decisions, some of an elementary nature and some more complex with potentially serious consequences. The choices we make can have long-lasting positive or negative effects. But in the end we are free to choose, assuming we have that privilege. What we choose can lead to triumph or defeat.

What necessitates much of our decision making is the stimuli that trigger our curiosity as goal-seeking beings. As adults it is expected that our accumulated knowledge and experience through years of living will ensure the likelihood of decisions with positive results. In the case of children, who haven't had the time to stockpile nearly the amount of knowledge and experience as their adult counterparts, one is concerned over decisions that they would make on matters that their curiosities draw them to. Will the by-product of their decisions threaten their well-being or that of others?

Our world is filled with wonder, beauty, mystery, and opportunity, all of which appeals to our curious natures. Conversely our world subjects us to the realities of danger, ugliness, and deceit as well. In a garden, weeds grow among flowers. Since they too may be colorfully adorned they often go undetected by the novice and succeed in their destruction. As adults we can be duped by the weeds of our world, thereby reducing the effectiveness of our knowledge and experience as weapons against poor decisions to that of a child.

While out in public one can often observe a child being directed along, hand in hand, by a parent. As the child's curiosity gets the better of him he pulls away in pursuit of the stimulus. The parent slackens a bit, allowing the child to investigate that which has his attention, however, still maintaining a firm grip. If the object of interest reveals itself to be a potential threat to the child's safety, the firm, protective, and loving hand of the parent gently tugs the child back to the security of the bosom. The child is confident in his exploration because he trusts that the loving hand will provide guidance and protection along the way.

Even as adults we know that our curiosity will at times lead us to difficult decisions. It is then that we too need proper guidance from without to protect us from poor choices that can be harmful. But if we put our trust solely in the guidance of worldly provisions then it is understandable that we cannot be completely assured. For even those of the greatest integrity and purest intentions can fail us, if only in death do they let us down.

Therefore as adults we too have need of that concerned, protective, supportive, and loving hand that guides us safely through the unexpected pitfalls of life whether by our own doing or other. Not just the hand of one in which we can place our belief, but the hand of

"The One" in which we confidently place our trust. My fervent hope is that we all will be... Found Always in Thy Hand.

"A Promise"

Upon a cross a debt was paid and a promise made.

For tortured souls enslaved.

From an empty tomb, as if a womb,
emerged the promise kept.

And by it we are saved.